TIME TRAVEL GUIDES

ANCIENT ROME

John Malam

www.raintree.co.uk/library
Visit our website to find out more information about Raintree books.

To order:

 Phone 44 (0) 1865 888112

 Send a fax to 44 (0) 1865 314091

 Visit the Raintree bookshop at www.raintree.co.uk/library to browse our catalogue and
order online.

First published in Great Britain by Raintree, Halley Court,
Jordan Hill, Oxford OX2 8EJ, part of Harcourt Education.
Raintree is a registered trademark of Harcourt Education
Ltd.

© Harcourt Education Ltd 2007
The moral right of the proprietor has been asserted.

Editorial: Sarah Shannon, Lucy Beevor,
and Harriet Milles
Design: Steve Mead and Geoff Ward
Picture Research: Ruth Blair
Illustrations: Eikon Illustration, Tim Slade
and Jeff Edwards
Production: Duncan Gilbert

Originated by Modern Age
Printed and bound in China by South China
Printing Company Ltd.

10 digit ISBN 1 4062 0599 0
13 digit ISBN 978 1 4062 0599 2

11 10 09 08 07
10 9 8 7 6 5 4 3 2 1

British Library Cataloguing in Publication Data
Malam, John, 1957-
Ancient Rome. - (Time travel guides)
1. Rome - Civilization - Juvenile literature
937
A full catalogue record for this book is available from the
British Library.

Acknowledgements
The publishers would like to thank the following for
permission to reproduce photographs:
AKG images **pp. 16**, **26** (Erich Lessing), **43** (Gilles
Mermet), **24**, **35** (Nimatallah), **15**, **34** (Peter Connolly),
9 (Pirozzi); Ancient Art & Architecture Collection
Ltd. **pp. 14**, **28**, **32**, **33**, **50–51**, **52**; Art Archive **pp. 49**
(Archaeological Museum, Corinth/Dagli Orti), **20–21**,
44–45, **54–55** (Bibliothèque des Arts Décoratifs, Paris/
Dagli Orti); **10**, **23**, **38–39** (Dagli Orti), **19** (Musée de
la Civilisation Gallo-Romaine, Lyons/Dagli Orti), **46**
(Museo Civico, Padua/Dagli Orti), **6–7**, **11**, **40**, **42**,
53 (Museo della Civilta Romana, Rome/Dagli Orti),
26–27 (Museo Nazionale, Palazzo Altemps, Rome/Dagli
Orti), **36** (Archaeological Museum, Madrid/Dagli
Orti), **8** (Archaeological Museum, Naples/Dagli Orti),
12 (Cathedral Museum, Ferrara/Dagli Orti), **30–31**
(Galleria Borghese, Rome/Dagli Orti), **25** (Jan Vinchon
Numismatist, Paris/Dagli Orti), **17** (Museo Prenestino,
Palestrina/Dagli Orti); Corbis **pp. 29** (Araldo de Luca), **18**
(Roger Wood).

Cover photograph of the Colosseum in Rome reproduced
with permission of Corbis/Richard T. Nowitz. Portrait
of the lawyer Terentius Neo and his wife reproduced
with permission of Werner Forman Archive/Museo
Archeologico Nazionale, Naples. Photograph of the head
of Octavian (Augustus) reproduced with permission of
Ancient Art & Architecture Collection Ltd./Prisma.

The publishers would like to thank Michael Vickers for
his assistance in the preparation of this book.

Every effort has been made to contact copyright holders
of any material reproduced in this book. Any omissions
will be rectified in subsequent printings if notice is given
to the publishers.

CONTENTS

Words that appear in the text in bold, **like this**, are explained in the Glossary.

N

W E

S

River Tiber

THE PANTHEON

THEATRE OF MARCELLUS

FORUM

THE COLOSSEUM

TIBERINA
ISLAND

CIRCUS MAXIMUS

BATHS OF CARACALLA

MAP OF ANCIENT ROME

Britain

Northern
Europe

France

Spain

Rome

Mediterranean Sea

Africa

◻ ROMAN EMPIRE

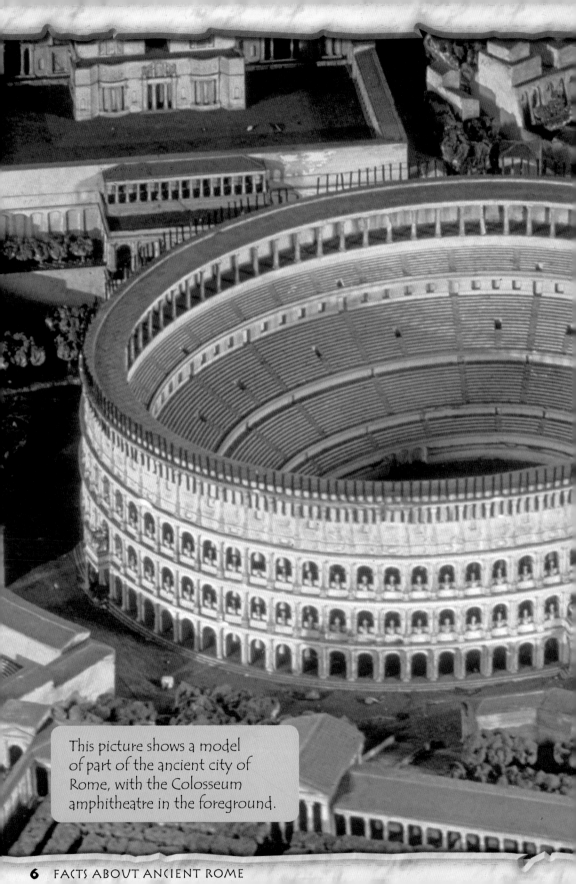

This picture shows a model
of part of the ancient city of
Rome, with the Colosseum
amphitheatre in the foreground.

CHAPTER 1

FACTS ABOUT ANCIENT ROME

You are about to go on the trip of a lifetime. Your destination is the city of ancient Rome, in the country of Italy. So, prepare to travel some 1,700 years back in time!

A good time to visit ancient Rome is in the early 4th century. This was when the city of Rome was at its greatest size. Since all of the city's major public buildings and squares have been built, you can explore them at your leisure. You will discover a wealthy, busy, **multicultural** city, and you will be made welcome. As you walk the city streets, accept the friendship of its people as they greet you with these words, spoken in the Latin language of the Romans: "*Salve, hospes!*" (Hello, stranger!). You should smile and reply: "*Salve!*" (Hello!)

THE BIRTH OF A GREAT CITY

In the modern world you might have heard someone say: "Rome was not built in a day." It's a way of saying that good things don't happen quickly – they take time. And so it is for ancient Rome. You'll be arriving there around AD 300, by which time the city will already be more than 1,000 years old! But how and when did this great city begin?

AENEAS, FATHER OF THE ANCIENT ROMAN PEOPLE

Ancient Romans tell a story that says Aeneas, a warrior, is the father of their people. His own city of Troy had been destroyed and he needed somewhere new to live. He travelled to Italy, where a **prophecy** about his future came true. He'd been told two things: that one day he'd eat the plate his food was served on, and that he'd make his new home at the place where he ate his plate.

In ancient times, food was often served on a piece of bread, and that was your plate. So, when Aeneas ate his bread plate, the prophecy came true. After that, he made Italy his home. All ancient Romans claim Aeneas is their **ancestor** and believe they can trace their **family tree** back to him.

This ancient painting shows Aeneas, the legendary founder of Rome. An arrow is being removed from his leg.

Babies Romulus and Remus being fed by the she-wolf.

ROMULUS AND REMUS

Another story describes the beginnings of Rome. Romulus and Remus were twins. When they were babies their great-uncle, King Amulius told his servants to drown the boys in the River Tiber. Luckily, the servants let their cot float away. A she-wolf found the babies and fed them with her own milk. Later, a shepherd took them home and raised them as his own sons. Romulus and Remus became brave men, and one day King Amulius asked to see them. Romulus killed the cruel king.

THE TRUE ORIGINS OF ANCIENT ROME

Ancient Romans believe that their city was founded on 21 April, 753 BC. This date was worked out by the Roman author Varro (116–27 BC). In fact, **archaeologists** from modern times have discovered that ancient Rome is older than this. The city actually began around 1000 BC as farming villages on the tops of seven low hills, which spread into the valleys. About 300 years later they joined up to make a small town, which grew into the present-day city. On your visit, don't offend the ancient Romans by telling them they've got the date wrong!

The twins built a city on a hill beside the River Tiber, but during an argument Romulus killed Remus. In honour of Romulus, the city was named Rome.

THE BUSY CAPITAL

Ancient Romans say their great city is *caput mundi*, which is Latin for "head" or "capital of the world". You might think this is a big claim to make – but it's true. When the ancient Romans talk about the world, they mean their **empire**. Rome is the capital of the Roman Empire, a vast area covering much of west Europe and parts of central Europe, north Africa, and east Asia. Around 50 million people live within the Roman Empire, and you can be certain that every one of them has heard of the city of Rome.

The Via Appia is a major road that approaches Rome from the south.

Like big cities of your own time, ancient Rome is a "people magnet", attracting visitors from every part of the empire. Ancient Rome's population is around one million. Most live here all year round, but others are visitors on business and, like you, some are tourists. This means the city is very multicultural, with a rich mix of races, languages, and religions.

LANGUAGES OF ANCIENT ROME

Latin is the official language of the Roman Empire, and you'll hear this spoken in many **dialects**. You'll also hear languages used by visitors from other lands. For example, Celtic and Gallic are spoken by people from the northern edge of the Roman Empire (Britain and France), and Aramaic and Hebrew is spoken by visitors from Judea (Israel). Listen out too for the languages of Greece, Egypt, Spain, Libya, and many more.

GETTING TO ANCIENT ROME

There's an old **proverb** that says "all roads lead to Rome", and they do. A network of around 80,000 km (50,000 miles) of roads crosses the Roman Empire. To travel to ancient Rome on foot, or by horse or carriage, keep to the major roads – they do indeed lead to Rome.

To find out how far you've travelled, visit the Roman **Forum** (see page 22). There you'll see the *Miliarium Aureum*, or Golden Milestone. On this gold-covered column are the names of major cities of the empire, with their distances from Rome.

If you're coming to ancient Rome by sea, your boat will dock at Ostia, the port of Rome, some 24 km (15 miles) southwest of the city. From there, you can take a river boat upstream via the River Tiber or travel by road on the *Via Campana*.

ANCIENT ROME STREET MAP

To guide you around the city's 90 kilometres (56 miles) of narrow streets and alleys, use the town plan known as the *Forma Urbis*. It is fixed to the wall of the Temple of Peace in the Forum of Vespasian. Measuring 18 metres by 13 metres (60 feet by 43 feet), it is made of 151 marble slabs. A detailed street plan is carved on the slabs, showing roads, temples, public buildings, houses, shops, water fountains, and public toilets. The picture on the right shows a fragment of the original *Forma Urbis*.

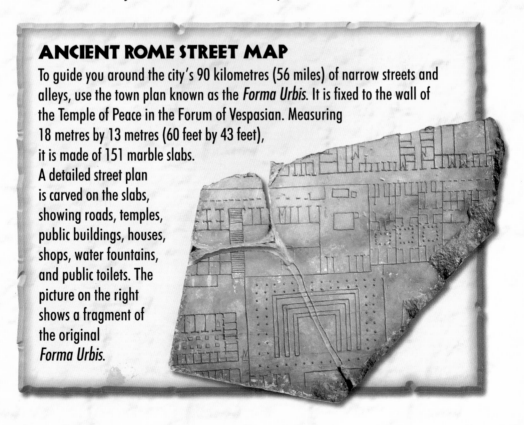

WHEN TO VISIT

Ancient Rome has something to offer the visitor all year round. If you like parties, then why not plan your visit at the same time as a festival? Most festivals are held in honour of Roman gods and goddesses. They're public holidays, when people relax and have fun. Romans have between 150 and 200 days of public holidays each year, so it's a wonder any work gets done!

THE FESTIVAL OF SATURNALIA

One of the highlights of the year is the festival of Saturnalia, held in December. It is the most important festival of the ancient Roman year and it lasts a week. On the first day an animal is **sacrificed** at the Temple of Saturn, in the main city square. Afterwards there's a huge feast. Look out for slaves pretending to be masters, and masters working as slaves – they change places at this time of year. Gambling, which is normally forbidden, is allowed. On the last day there's a fair with market stalls where people buy small gifts for each other. Parents give money to their children to buy presents for their friends.

During the festival of Saturnalia, people give one another gifts. These could be wax candles or pottery figures like the one of the god Saturn in this picture.

MODERN LINKS

The festival of Saturnalia, which is **pagan**, has a link with the modern world. The early leaders of the Christian Church turned it into the Christian festival of 25 December – the celebration of the birth of Jesus Christ.

THE FESTIVAL OF PARILIA

Lots of festivals involve the sacrifice of animals, but if you don't like the sight of blood then plan your visit for the April festival of Parilia. It's in honour of Rome's birthday, and it also asks the gods to protect farmers and their animals. You'll see bonfires of straw, and ashes from a calf sacrificed in March will be thrown onto the fires, as will **sulphur** and the plants pine, laurel, and juniper. The air will be smoky and smelly, and the straw will crackle as it burns. If you take part, you'll be expected to jump through the flames and then drink milk.

THE WEATHER IN ANCIENT ROME

Seasons

Spring (March–May): warm and showery
Summer (June–August): very hot and dry
Autumn (September–November): warm and rainy
Winter (December–February): cold

Average daytime temperature

January: 5°C–11°C (40°F–52°F)
July: 20°C–30°C (67°F–87°F)
September: 17°C–26°C (62°F–79°F)

Average rainfall

January: 71 mm (2.8 in)
July: 15 mm (0.6 in)
September: 63 mm (2.5 in)

Average days of sunshine

January: 7 sunny days out of 31
July: 26 sunny days out of 31
September: 24 sunny days out of 30

Average days of rain

January: 8 rainy days out of 31
July: 1 rainy day out of 31
September: 5 rainy days out of 30

WHERE TO STAY

There's no shortage of accommodation in ancient Rome, so it shouldn't take you too long to find a room or house to stay in. But be prepared for a shock – some of the places you'll be offered will be in a dreadful condition.

ACCOMMODATION ON A BUDGET

If you're on a budget, rent an apartment in one of the city's many multi-storey housing blocks (*insulae*), some of which have five storeys and are 18 metres (60 feet) high. According to a recent survey, the city has more

If you rent a house, its rooms will be set around a private garden.

than 46,000 one-roomed apartments. Although they might be basic and cheap, none of them has running water or cooking facilities, and the communal toilets are not for the squeamish (see box). The blocks they are in are overcrowded, with whole families living in the small rooms. They're noisy, dirty places, where fires and disease can spread quickly.

ANCIENT ROMAN HOMES

If you've come to ancient Rome with a lot of money, then rent a house (*domus*), perhaps from a family while they are away from the city. It will have an entrance hall, several bedrooms, and a dining room, arranged around a garden and a courtyard. In the courtyard there will be a well for fresh water and a hearth for cooking food. Most houses are single-storey dwellings, with all rooms at ground level. The house will be clean, comfortable, and private – the total opposite of an apartment.

GOING TO THE TOILET

If you stay in a house you'll have a cesspit in the garden or yard. It's a deep hole into which you empty the contents of your chamber pot. If you are in an apartment, you will have to use one of the block's toilet pipes. Be warned — there will be hundreds of people living in the block, and the "rotten egg" stench from the pipes is very strong. The pipes empty into mega-cesspits on the ground. Every so often the pits are emptied and the muck is spread over fields, making farmers' crops grow better.

BENEATH THE CITY STREETS

Running under the city is the *Cloaca Maxima*, or "great drain". It's the city's main sewer, snaking its way beneath the streets for 900 metres (2,950 feet), flushing raw sewage from toilets and gutters into the River Tiber (so avoid swimming there!). In places the sewer tunnel is 4 metres (13 feet) high and 3 metres (10 feet) wide. It is a wonder of ancient Roman engineering, and parts of it are still in use in the 21st century.

There is no privacy in Roman public toilets.

FOOD AND DRINK

You won't go hungry or thirsty on your visit, as you will find bakeries, bars, taverns, and restaurants on most city streets. For a hot snack, such as sausages, pies, and stews, visit a *popina* or a *thermopolium*. Whatever you choose, be prepared for it to be spiced with pepper, sprinkled with sour vinegar, or smothered in salty fish sauce (*garum*). Cakes and pastries taste sweet as they have lots of honey in them.

Mealtimes will be different from what you are used to. Ancient Romans tend to skip breakfast (*ientaculum*) or eat a light snack of bread, cheese, fruit, and water. The midday meal (*prandium*) is also small – a little hot-cooked meat or fish, eaten with bread and washed down with wine. The day's main meal (*cena*) is eaten at about 3.00 p.m. and, if it's a **banquet**, will last for several hours (see box).

WINE AND WATER

Don't be surprised to see wine being drunk in great quantities. In some parts of the city, wine is safer to drink than water! Wine is not drunk neat. Instead, it's mixed with water, and might be flavoured with herbs, honey, or pine **resin**. As for fresh water, you will find more than 1,300 fountains across the city.

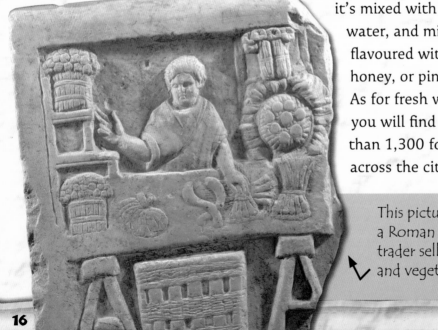

This picture shows a Roman market trader selling fruit and vegetables.

✍ A musician will entertain you as you tuck into a banquet.

KNOW YOUR TABLE MANNERS

At a banquet, it is good manners to lie on one of the low couches set out around the table. Lie on your left side propped up on your elbow, and spread a napkin in front of you to catch bits that fall. Before the meal and between each course, wash your hands, or let a servant do it for you. When you feel full, it is good manners to belch and break wind. Some ancient Romans make room for more food by making themselves sick. They leave the table and go into a small side room, where they tickle the inside of their throats with a feather. After the meal your host will expect you to stay for games and songs.

BIG BANQUET

What might you eat if you're invited to a banquet? For the first course (*gustatio*) you will dine on shellfish and oysters in garlic sauce, snails in their shells, boiled eggs, olives, figs, lettuce, and sweet wine. For the main course (*caput cenae*), you will be served with slices of roast boar stuffed with sausages and egg yolks, stuffed dormice in honey sauce, peacocks, fish, cabbage, and scented wine. For dessert (*secunda mensa*), you will have a choice of fresh fruit and nuts, or cakes and honeyed wine.

WHAT TO WEAR

Clothes say a lot about a person's status in ancient Rome, as the rich and poor dress very differently. You may want to pay careful attention to what you wear on your visit.

CLOTHES FOR MEN AND BOYS

The tunic has become the most popular piece of clothing for men and boys. It's made from itchy wool, but the wealthy prefer it in linen or even silk. Whatever you do, don't forget to wear a belt around your waist, or people will think you're not dressed properly. Sleeves come in and out of fashion. In the early 4th century the style is for sleeveless tunics. A tunic can be plain, or decorated with a purple stripe from shoulder to hem.

WHAT NOT TO WEAR

Clothes quickly come in and go out of fashion in ancient Rome! The **toga** was once the standard item of clothing for men and boys (see the man seated in the picture), but now you'll only see it worn by city officials, **magistrates**, and politicians. For women, it's the *stola* that's old-fashioned. Once, every woman in ancient Rome wore one of these ankle-length pleated gowns. Now they prefer a simpler no-fuss tunic.

If you feel cold, wear several layers of tunics or put a cloak on. Cloaks have a hood to keep your head dry in the rain – or maybe you'd rather wear a wide-brimmed hat. Wear leather sandals indoors and leather ankle boots outside. If you wear wooden-soled shoes (like clogs), people will think you're a peasant or a slave.

FASHIONS FOR WOMEN AND GIRLS

Plain or stripy tunics are fashionable, worn as ankle-length garments with sleeves and a belt. Women's leather shoes are softer and coloured red. Wealthy families fasten pearls to their shoes. There are no hats for women, so they pull their cloaks over their heads if it starts to rain. If you're so rich that you can afford a personal slave, he or she will protect you from the weather with a parasol.

HAIRSTYLES AND BEARDS

Men – don't come to ancient Rome with hairy chins and cheeks! In the early 4th century, beards are out of fashion, unless you're a criminal or mourning someone who has died. You should also have short, straight hair – the curly Roman hairstyles are no longer considered "manly".

WOMEN'S HAIRSTYLES

In the past, women spent ages combing and curling their long hair into high crests, but in the early 4th century they prefer to quickly comb it straight back into a bun. If you've got black or brown hair, have a think about dyeing the colour to blonde, which is the current fashion.

Roman women have pierced ears and wear dangly earrings.

The Forum is the symbol of ancient Rome's power and glory.

CHAPTER 2

PLACES TO VISIT

There's so much to see in ancient Rome that you won't know what to visit first! The city has eleven town squares, eleven big bathhouses (and 856 smaller ones!), ten basilicas (shopping centres with offices and law courts), and twenty-eight libraries. A good place to begin your sightseeing is in the *Forum Romanum* – the historic centre of ancient Rome and the centre of the Roman Empire. From there you'll be within easy reach of ancient Rome's shops and markets, and a short walk from the Pantheon building where you can pay your respects to the Romans' gods and goddesses. You'll be doing a lot of walking, so at the end of the day why not pamper yourself with a massage at the baths or a dip in the pools?

THE ROMAN FORUM

Of all the city's squares, the *Forum Romanum* (Roman Forum) is the one to see. It's sometimes called the Great Forum, but it's not so great in size – it's a rather small, narrow space, about 100 metres by 70 metres (320 feet by 230 feet). Even so, this little square is the symbol of Roman power and glory. The Forum has always been the nerve centre of ancient Rome – the place where politicians, lawyers, and soldiers make great speeches. It's also been used for processions, trials, elections, banquets, **gladiatorial** games, political meetings, and religious ceremonies. All of ancient Rome's roads meet here, at the *Miliarium Aureum*, or Golden Milestone (see page 11).

The *Forum Romanum* is hemmed in on all sides by government buildings, law courts, **temples**, basilicas (shopping centres), archways, statues, and columns. In the **arcades** of the basilicas around the edge of the square, bankers, money-lenders, silversmiths, food sellers, and pickpockets conduct their work.

As the city and the Roman Empire grew, the *Forum Romanum* became too small for all the work that had to be done in its cramped surroundings. The solution was to build more town squares, and that's why ancient Rome now has so many forums.

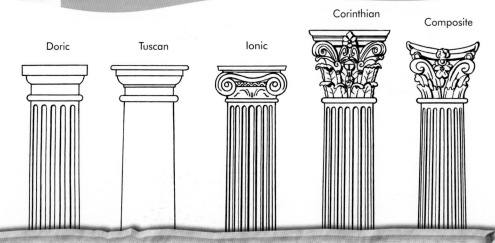

Columns were an important architectural feature in ancient Rome. This picture shows the five main styles.

Doric   Tuscan   Ionic   Corinthian   Composite

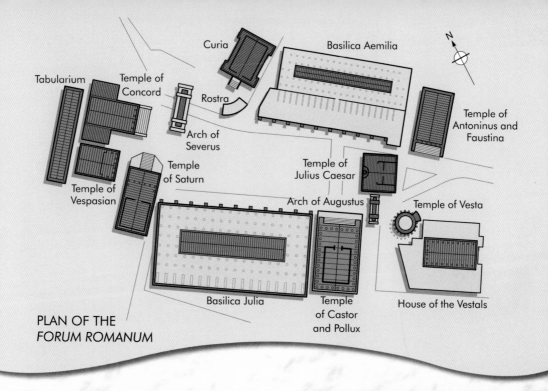

Curia
Basilica Aemilia
N

Tabularium
Temple of Concord
Rostra
Temple of Antoninus and Faustina

Arch of Severus

Temple of Saturn
Temple of Julius Caesar
Temple of Vesta

Temple of Vespasian
Arch of Augustus

Basilica Julia
Temple of Castor and Pollux
House of the Vestals

PLAN OF THE
FORUM ROMANUM

THE TEMPLE OF VESTA

You'll find this ancient circular temple close to the centre of the Forum. It's the most important temple in the whole of ancient Rome and is dedicated to the goddess Vesta. She is the protector of the home and its hearth, and her temple is circular to remind Romans of the round huts their ancestors lived in long ago. Inside the temple is Rome's **sacred** flame. It burns day and night, and is attended to by the six Vestal Virgins. It is the duty of these priestesses to keep the fire burning – should they let the flame die then this signals danger for Rome.

Most Roman temples are rectangular, but the Temple of Vesta is circular.

This stone sculpture shows customers at a fabric shop buying textiles and pillows.

SHOPS AND MARKETS

Come to ancient Rome and spend, spend, spend! Everywhere you turn you'll see shops and stalls. The city even has a multi-storey shopping centre where you'll find goods of every description.

For your everyday needs, try the open-fronted shops on the ground floor of the city's apartment blocks. At the back of the shops are work spaces where the shopkeepers make or store their goods. These are excellent places to buy your daily bread and wine, as well as olive oil, lamps, meat, fish, pots and pans, fabrics for clothes, and cheap jewellery.

Also look out for temporary stalls, usually set up by farmers on the pavements. When you're choosing your fruits and vegetables, remember that they were growing in the farmer's fields and orchards just a few hours earlier. You can't get much fresher than that! You'll need to take your own basket to hold your shopping, and if you buy oil or wine, remember to take an empty jar for the shopkeeper to fill.

If you're looking for a luxury item to take home, go to the *Forum Romanum* or one of the other squares. In these places you'll find shops and stalls selling gold and silver jewellery, carved ivory goods, perfume, and books, each one neatly handwritten onto a long roll of paper.

MONEY AND MONEY-LENDERS

Pay for your shopping with gold or bronze coins – but make sure you use the right ones. In the early 4th century, the only coins to use are ones with a picture of Emperor Constantine on the front. You will probably see lots of coins with pictures of ancient Rome's earlier emperors, but these are now worthless.

If you run out of money, think carefully before you approach a money-lender. He'll lend you the money you need, but he will ask you to pay it back with an extra amount added on. If you're not careful, you could end up in debt, owing more than you can ever afford to pay.

SLAVES FOR SALE
Like it or not, the ancient Romans buy and sell slaves. Some are prisoners of war, some are criminals, and others are people who have got themselves into debt. Ancient Rome's slave market is in the *Forum Romanum*. If you're there at sale time, you'll see the unfortunate souls standing on platforms while people bid in an **auction** to buy them.

These coins show the head of the emperor Constantine.

THE PANTHEON

No visit to ancient Rome is complete until you've seen the Pantheon. It was built between AD 118 and AD 125 and is a masterpiece of Roman architecture. You'll find it in the *Campus Martius* district in the northwest of the city, tucked into a wide bend of the River Tiber.

The Pantheon is a temple to all the gods and goddesses of ancient Rome, whereas other Roman temples are dedicated to single deities.

Inside the Pantheon, looking up to the "eye" in the roof.

As you enter the building you'll step into the world's biggest domed structure – a record that won't be broken for more than 1,000 years! The top of the great dome is 43 metres (140 feet) from the ground. Daylight pours in through a wide hole in the centre of the roof, 9 metres (30 feet) across. This is the *oculus* or "eye". On a bright day the sun's rays will reach into the darkest corners of the Pantheon's interior. They light up the **niches** around the walls, where statues of gods and goddesses stand.

HOUSES FOR THE GODS

The ancient Romans see gods and goddesses as powerful beings that control every aspect of daily life (see box). A temple is a god's home on Earth. Inside it is a sacred statue, and the Romans are convinced that the god's spirit actually lives within it.

You'll see people leaving gifts for the gods at their temples, from a few crumbs of bread to a sheep or a goat (it will be sacrificed on the god's **altar**). In return for these offerings, people hope the gods will help them.

ROMAN GODS AND GODDESSES

The twelve most important gods and goddesses are:

- **Apollo** – god of prophecy and healing
- **Ceres** – goddess of agriculture
- **Diana** – goddess of the moon and hunting
- **Juno** – goddess of women and marriage; queen of the gods, married to Jupiter
- **Jupiter** – god of the heavens and weather; king of the gods, married to Juno
- **Mars** – god of war
- **Mercury** – god of communications and travellers
- **Minerva** – goddess of wisdom
- **Neptune** – god of the oceans and earthquakes (see picture on right).
- **Venu** – goddess of love
- **Vesta** – goddess of the home and hearth
- **Vulcan** – god of fire and **blacksmiths**

CHRISTIANS ARE WELCOME!

If you're a Christian you might feel nervous about travelling to ancient Rome. After all, it was the Romans who executed Jesus Christ nearly 300 years ago, and there have been times when Christians have been **persecuted** for their beliefs. But you need not worry any more. In AD 313, Emperor Constantine allows Christians to practise their religion without fear.

BENE LAVA! (HAVE A GOOD BATH)

At the end of a tiring day, what could be better than a visit to the baths? In ancient Rome there are many large and small baths to choose from, where you can relax with a massage, take a dip in the pools, exercise in the gymnasium, and meet friends.

THE BATHS OF CARACALLA

For the ultimate experience, look no further than the Baths of Caracalla, which are the grandest in ancient Rome. You'll find them in the south of the city, near the main road known as the *Via Appia*. They're a massive complex of buildings, begun around AD 200 during the reign of Emperor Caracalla. They are so big that up to 2,500 people can enjoy themselves there at any one time. But please note that mixed bathing is not allowed! Women, the elderly, and the disabled use the baths in the morning, and men in the afternoon.

WHO'S WHO AT THE BATHS?

- **Capsarii** – changing room attendants who will look after your clothes.
- **Alipili** – hair-removers who will cut, shave, and pluck out your hair.
- **Aliptae** – body-scrapers who will use oil to clean your grimy body.
- **Tractatores** – massage experts who rub oils into your aching body.
- **Unctores** – perfume sellers whose scented oils will make you smell nice.

Fill a flask with oil, and use it at the baths.

CENTRAL HEATING

As you sweat in the *sudatorium* (steam room), or swim in the *tepidarium* (heated pool), you might wonder where the heat comes from. For the Baths of Caracalla, there are 5 kilometres (3 miles) of tunnels beneath the floors and behind the walls of the baths, which bring in hot air from wood-burning furnaces. The hot air heats the water, produces steam for the sweat rooms, and keeps the building warm and cosy.

Millions of Romans have cleaned themselves at the Baths of Caracalla.

VISITING THE ANCIENT ROMAN BATHS

When you visit the baths, you will need to take your own bathing equipment – a flask of oil, a scraper, a comb, and linen or woollen towels. Then:

1 Go to the *apodyterium* (the changing room) and remove your clothes – all of them!
2 Go to the *sudatorium*. Sit inside this small room where hot steam will make you sweat, forcing grime out of your skin.
3 Go to the *caldarium*. Another hot room, where you should rub warm oil into your skin, then scrape it off with a *strigil* (scraper). Or you could let a body-scraper do this for you.
4 Go to the *tepidarium*. Cool down by soaking yourself in the lukewarm pool in this room.
5 Go to the *frigidarium*. Now plunge into this room's cold pool and have a swim.
6 Go to the *unctuarium*. Have a massage with perfumed oils then get dressed.
7 Don't rush off! – buy something to eat from the cake and sausage sellers and chat with friends whilst you watch others exercising.

Gladiator fights are an extremely popular spectator sport in ancient Rome!

CHAPTER 3

FUN AND GAMES

Ancient Rome is well known for its different types of entertainment, so there is something to suit all tastes. If you fancy the thrills and spills of **chariot** racing, then head off to the *Circus Maximus*, which is the city's biggest racetrack. Or maybe you prefer to see the beast-fighters and gladiators in blood-spilling action in the Colosseum arena? But if neither of these take your fancy, there's always the theatre, where Roman actors will make you laugh out loud or cry into your handkerchief.

A modern photo of the ruins of the Theatre of Marcellus – with houses added at the top!

OFF TO THE THEATRE!

Theatres are popular with visitors and the people of ancient Rome. They're open-air buildings in the shape of a semi-circle. The audience sits in rows as actors perform on the stage in front of them. In most plays, all the parts are played by men – even the parts of women!

ANCIENT ROME'S THEATRES

If you're in ancient Rome at the time of a public holiday, then follow the crowds as they head to the west end of the city. Here you'll find the theatre district, in the Campus Martius area. Close together are three major theatres – the Theatre of Pompey, the Theatre of Balbus, and best of all, the magnificent Theatre of Marcellus.

The Theatre of Marcellus is Rome's premier theatre, with room for about 20,000 people. Performances are staged in the afternoon, and it's best to arrive early to be sure of getting a seat. The good news is that it's free to watch a play (all forms of public entertainment are free). The bad news is that the stone seats are incredibly uncomfortable, so take a soft cushion to sit on!

Tickets (small squares or discs made from bone or ivory) are handed out by city officials, and they're always in short supply. Please note that men and women do not sit together – women have their own seats at the back, behind the men. The front few rows are reserved for the emperor, senators, and the rich.

ACTORS AND PLAYS

There are two main types of play: comedies and tragedies. You'll soon know which type you're watching from the happy or sad face masks the actors wear – happy masks for comedy and sad masks for tragedy. Also, a brown mask means the actor is playing the part of a man, while a white mask shows he is acting as a woman. An actor playing the part of an old man will wear white clothes, whereas for a youth he will wear clothes of many colours. For a rich person he will wear purple, and for a poor person he will wear red.

This mask would be worn by an actor playing the part of a wrinkled old man in a comedy.

CHEER THE CHARIOTS!

To see chariot racing and the finest racehorses in action, go to one of ancient Rome's four racetracks, known as *circuses*. By far the best is *Circus Maximus* ("Great Circus"), in the south of the city. It's well-named as it's the biggest racetrack in the whole of the ancient Roman world, measuring 600 metres (1,970 feet) in length and 200 metres (650 feet) in width.

The *Circus Maximus* is a place of thrills and spills.

On a race day up to 200,000 spectators will be seated around the track. Men and women are allowed to sit together. Entry is free, and the stadium starts to fill up quickly from dawn, so aim to arrive early. Outside the entrances you will see market traders selling food, so buy a lunchtime snack on your way inside.

CHOOSE YOUR TEAM

Charioteers belong to racing-clubs. There are four clubs, and the charioteers (and their fans) wear the colours of their team:
- Reds – the Russata team
- Whites – the Albata team
- Blues – the Veneta team
- Greens – the Prasina team

An ancient Roman race-meeting is a team sport, and spectators go to the races hoping to see their team win. Choose a team (see box), and be sure to wear something with your team's colour on it to show who you support.

A DAY AT THE RACES

The meeting begins with a parade, which is your chance to view the charioteers. Then the chariots line up at the starting boxes. When the race starter drops a white cloth, they're off! As many as twelve chariots take part in a race, hurtling anti-clockwise around the track at speeds of up to 75 kph (46 mph) for seven laps, covering a distance of about 5.2 kilometres (3.2 miles).

Watch out for crashes and pile-ups at either end of the track, where the bends are tight. Chariot-racing is dangerous, and horses and drivers can be seriously injured or killed. This is bad news for them, but the ancient Romans find it exciting.

A race will be over in less than ten minutes. Attendants will then tidy the track ready for the next race. The biggest race-meetings at the *Circus Maximus* have 24 races a day, involving around 1,000 horses. In between races, acrobats will entertain you as they race at full speed and jump from one horse to the next.

FAMOUS CHARIOTEERS

Charioteers are the sporting stars of the day, and the most popular have their own fan clubs. Here are three of the most famous:

- Pompeius Musclosus – won 3,559 races
- Scorpus – won 2,048 races
- Diocles – won 1,462 races

The winner of a chariot race holds a palm frond as a sign of victory.

GO TO THE GAMES!

For the greatest show in town, the games are the place to be – but not if you might faint at the sight of blood. Ancient Roman games, *ludi*, are all about physical combat – men fighting wild animals, the execution of criminals, and gladiatorial contests. This all happens inside the massive Flavian Amphitheatre, better known in your time as the Colosseum. It's ancient Rome's ultimate killing ground in the very heart of the city.

In ancient Rome, gladiators are similar to warriors, top atheletes, and movie stars all in one!

THE GAMES ARE COMING!

You'll know when the games are coming to town because a few days before they arrive, notices will be painted on the walls of buildings. Entry is free, and to get in you'll need an admission ticket. They are handed out by city officials and will be snapped up quickly.

A DAY AT THE GAMES
- **Morning**: animal hunts, when lions, tigers, rhinoceroses, and other wild beasts are killed by animal hunters.
- **Midday**: execution of criminals, when **condemned** men and women are fed to the beasts.
- **Afternoon**: gladiatorial contests, when pairs of men fight to the death.

WATCHING THE ACTION

On the day of the games, enter the Colosseum by one of the 76 public entrances, then make your way up to your seat (the row and seat number are marked on your ticket). You'll be one of 50,000 excited and noisy people all looking down to the sandy floor where the games will be staged. (The sand soaks up the blood.) The games last all day without a stop, so take food and drink with you.

SIGN LANGUAGE

When a defeated gladiator falls to the ground, his opponent will stand over him, ready to finish him off – but only if the crowd agrees. The crowd will signal with their thumbs (up or down), or call out to show whether the gladiator should kill the loser or let him go. Useful phrases to call out are:
- *Hoc habet!* – Get him!
- *Mitte!* – Let him go!
- *Iugula!* – Kill him!

These ruins are all that is left of the once magnificent Roman Forum.

CHAPTER 4

GOVERNING THE CITY

As you explore the buildings and attractions of ancient Rome, take time to stop and think about how this magnificent city works. Who are the people in power? What are the laws and how are they kept? These are important questions. The answers to them will help you understand how ancient Rome has come to be the greatest place on Earth.

RULERS OF ANCIENT ROME

In the beginning, ancient Rome was ruled by kings. Unfortunately they let power go to their heads and were cruel to ordinary people. Rome's last king was overthrown in 509 BC, after which a new type of government, called a **republic**, came to power.

During the first years of the Republic, ancient Rome was ruled by the Senate. This was a group of elected officials, or **senators**. They decided how the city should be organized and run, made laws, and controlled the army. However, it was not a perfect system. When a powerful **general** named Julius Caesar became dictator (sole ruler) for life, it wasn't much better than having a king in charge. So, a group of senators **assassinated** Caesar. After this, a power struggle broke out. The eventual winner was Caesar's great nephew, Octavian. In 27 BC he changed his name to Augustus, meaning "revered", and called himself *imperator*, from which comes the word "emperor". Augustus was Rome's first emperor and he handed power back to the Senate.

A marble statue of the emperor Augustus. He is remembered as a good ruler.

GOOD AND BAD EMPERORS

By the 4th century there has been a long line of men (never women) who have ruled ancient Rome, starting with Emperor Augustus. The emperors have been a real mix of good and bad guys:

Emperor	Reigned	Good or bad?	Reason
Augustus	27 BC–AD 14	Good	Caring emperor who began to rebuild ancient Rome.
Caligula	AD 37–41	Bad	Wasted money and thought he was a god.
Nero	AD 54–68	Bad	Murdered his mother and persecuted Christians.
Trajan	AD 98–117	Good	Expanded the Roman Empire to its greatest size.
Marcus Aurelius	AD 161–180	Good	A thoughtful and popular emperor.
Commodus	AD 180–192	Bad	Tried to rename ancient Rome *Commodiana*, after himself.

THE EMPEROR'S BODYGUARD

The emperor has his own personal army, known as the Praetorian Guard. They are the only soldiers allowed into the city. They have a large camp on the northeast outskirts, which can house as many as 10,000 Praetorians.

The Praetorian Guards' job is to protect the emperor and the city of Rome from danger – and they have been doing this ever since Emperor Augustus created them. However, later emperors depend on the Praetorians less and less.

LAW AND ORDER

The ancient Romans take great pride in their legal system, which they believe is the fairest in the world. It's taken hundreds of years for the ancient Romans to work out their laws, which form rules for all law-abiding people to follow – including you!

A SYSTEM OF PUNISHMENTS

If you do break the law, here is what could happen to you:

For a small everyday crime, such as theft, it is up to your victim, the victim's family and friends, neighbours, or passers-by, to arrest you and decide your fate (you might be given a fine or a flogging). The idea is that people should be able to help each other in sorting out right from wrong.

If you are accused of a serious crime, such as murder or treason (an offence against the state), you can expect to be sent to court for trial. If you refuse to go, force can be used to get you there. The court usually meets in a court house in the Roman Forum (see page 22), where a **jury** will listen to the facts of the case and then decide what should happen to you. If you are found not guilty, you will be free to leave.

This sculpture shows a group of officials, or senators. The laws of ancient Rome are decided by elected senators.

A condemned man is killed by a wild animal.

However, if the jury decides you are guilty as charged, you can expect the punishment to fit the crime. You could be exiled from the city (sent to a faraway part of the Roman Empire), or made to do hard labour working in the mines or rowing a warship. The ultimate punishment is the death sentence – beheading, **impalement** on a stake, or being savaged by wild animals in the arena (see page 36). The golden rule as a visitor to the city is: stay out of trouble!

FIREMEN ACTING AS POLICEMEN

Strictly speaking, there is no such thing as a police force in ancient Rome (this is a modern invention). However, the city does have a fire brigade known as the *vigiles*, made up of about 7,000 freed slaves. Their main duty is to put out fires and demolish buildings to prevent fires from spreading, but the government also uses them to keep order on the streets. If you see a big disturbance, such as a riot, don't get involved. The government will send in the *vigiles*, or even the Praetorian Guard (see page 41), to break things up with extreme force.

No expense has been spared in building or decorating this magnificent villa.

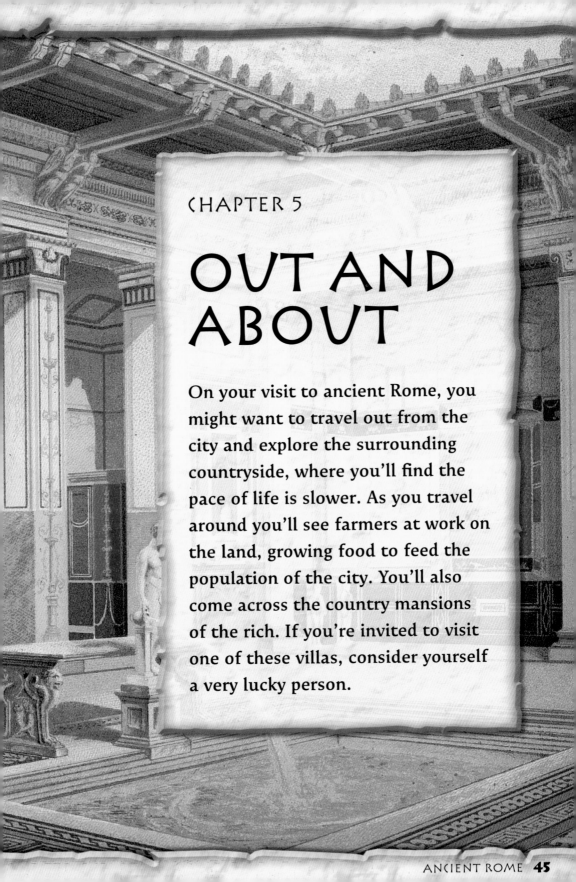

CHAPTER 5

OUT AND ABOUT

On your visit to ancient Rome, you might want to travel out from the city and explore the surrounding countryside, where you'll find the pace of life is slower. As you travel around you'll see farmers at work on the land, growing food to feed the population of the city. You'll also come across the country mansions of the rich. If you're invited to visit one of these villas, consider yourself a very lucky person.

CHOOSE YOUR TRANSPORT

For a trip into the country you'll need to choose a suitable form of transport. The easiest and cheapest way to travel is by walking – but it will take a long time to get very far on foot. Many travellers rent or buy a horse from stables in the city. If you do this, make sure your animal is in good condition and is not **lame**. Some horse-traders buy old or injured horses from the chariot races (see pages 34–35), then charge high prices to unsuspecting travellers. If you can't afford a horse, make do with a mule or even a donkey.

CARRIAGES

If you don't know how to ride a horse, don't panic – take a carriage. It will cost more than a horse, but it will be a lot more comfortable. You'll find there is a choice of carriages.

A husband, wife, and their driver travelling in a horse-drawn carriage.

The best carriage is a four-wheeled vehicle called a *carruca*, which is pulled by two horses. It doesn't go very fast, covering no more than 40 kilometres (25 miles) in a day (you could walk further than this!), but it is the height of luxury. It comes with its own driver and there's plenty of room for you and your luggage. Lie down and have a nap if you're sleepy, or just admire the countryside from the window.

A BED FOR THE NIGHT

It's not advisable to travel at night. Because there are no lights on the roads, horses, drivers, and bearers will not be able to see their way ahead. Away from the main roads, the tracks are full of potholes, and there is the constant danger of bandits, who will be keen to steal your money – and your clothes! Make sure you find an inn where you'll be able to rest for the night.

If it's speed you want, then choose a two-wheeled carriage called a *cisium*, pulled by two horses. It also comes with a driver, and he'll work hard to keep the horses galloping quickly along the road. If you're travelling a long distance, the driver will stop at a roadside inn to change the tired horses for fresh ones. This way you'll be able to cover around 80 kilometres (50 miles) in ten hours.

TRAVEL IN STYLE

If you're not in a hurry, you'll be able to hire a bunch of bearers who will carry you by **litter**, which is basically a wooden box with a seat, windows, and curtains. The smartest and best bearers are from Bithynia, which is a province in the eastern part of the Roman Empire (where northern Turkey is today). You'll need about eight bearers. It's the slowest form of land transport, but it's got style and is favoured by emperors and the rich.

VISIT A VILLA

The humble farmers who sell their produce in the markets of ancient Rome have something in common with the city's richest citizens – they both have villas in the countryside. But the farmer's villa is the complete opposite to the villa of a rich man. While the farmer's villa is a working farm, the rich man's villa is his country mansion or holiday home, where he goes to escape from the hustle and bustle of the big city.

Simple farm villa

LIVING IN LUXURY

If you are invited to visit a rich man's villa, you'll be treated as an honoured guest. The largest villas are like self-contained mini-villages, complete with bakeries, bath-houses, dining rooms, bedrooms, courtyards, storerooms, and gardens. The owner may be out working in the city when you arrive. However, his servants will see to your every need. Admire the villa's fine wall paintings and **mosaics** (see box). Then a servant will call you for a good meal at the owner's table. Afterwards, stroll around the pretty garden. When it's time for bed, a servant will show you to your room.

Rich man's villa

PICTURES IN STONE

You can judge how rich a villa owner is by the quality of his mosaics. These are pictures on the floors and walls made from small cubes (*tesserae*) of coloured stone, and sometimes pottery and glass. The most expensive mosaics are made from the tiniest cubes — cheaper pictures are made from bigger, chunkier cubes. An expensive mosaic uses lots of colours and will make a detailed picture, whereas a cheaper mosaic uses fewer colours to produce simple patterns.

A boy is given a school lesson by his teacher.

CHAPTER 6

CHILDREN IN ANCIENT ROME

The city of ancient Rome is not just for adults – it's a great place for children to live in. Ancient Roman children play a lot of different games. They also have toys, keep pets, and many of them go to school, particularly boys from rich families. To help you enjoy your trip, here's an insight into what the lives of ancient Roman boys and girls are like.

FROM TOYS TO TEACHERS

For toys, children play with rag dolls and model animals made from pottery. They have hobby-horses, spinning tops and hoops, and building bricks. Marbles made from balls of baked clay and marble stone are rolled along the ground. Miniature chariots pulled by strings (or pet mice) are raced around makeshift tracks. Other pets are cats, dogs, and caged birds such as blackbirds. Like children of today, ancient Roman boys and girls play dressing-up games when they pretend to be grown-ups.

THE GAME OF MICARE OR MORA

Every child in ancient Rome knows how to play the "flashing fingers" game, so make sure you know the rules:

1 Stand in front of your opponent.
2 On the count of three, both of you raise your right hands with some fingers outstretched.
3 At the same time as you raise your hands, you each call out a number from 0 to 10.
4 If your number matches the number of fingers that both you and your opponent showed, score a point.
5 First one to reach an agreed number of points wins the game.

HEADS OR SHIPS?

When children need to decide who goes first in a game, they toss an old coin and call out "capita" ("heads") or "navia" ("ships"). Old coins have a picture of a ship on the "tail" side. In the AD 300s they cannot be used as money — but they are great for games!

The game of merels is still played today and is known as "Nine Men's Morris".

GOING TO SCHOOL

In ancient Rome, boys from rich families go to school, but boys from poor families don't. Girls don't go to school at all, but stay at home where they learn how to cook, make clothes, and look after the family.

Boys sent to school learn how to read and write in Latin and Greek, they recite texts to their teachers, and study arithmetic, history, and **astronomy**. The school day starts at dawn and finishes in the early afternoon, before the day gets too hot. Teachers are tough, and will punish a boy who behaves badly, forgets his lines, or gives the wrong answer, by hitting him with a leather strap or cane stick. You have been warned!

These children are rolling nuts in a game.

WHEN CHILDHOOD ENDS

A boy becomes a man on his 16th birthday. It is the most important day of his life, and to mark his "coming of age" he takes part in a ceremony. He gives up his *bulla* (**lucky charm**) that he might have worn throughout his childhood, together with his *toga praetexta* (a white garment for boys). From then on he wears a man's clothes (see page 18), and is allowed to do all the things a man can do.

A girl comes of age when she is about 14 years old. She is then expected to give up her childhood toys, get married, and start a family of her own.

A 20th-century artist's impression of the busy west side of the Forum.

CHAPTER 7

ANCIENT ROME FACTS AND FIGURES

LATIN PHRASEBOOK

For visitors who cannot understand Latin, these words and phrases will come in useful. As for pronunciation, if you say every letter in the word as it is written, you won't go far wrong. Note, however, that "c" should sound like a "k", and "v" should sound like a "w".

GENERAL LATIN PHRASES

Hello	*Salve* (but *Salvete* if you are talking to more than one person)
Goodbye	*Vale* (but *Valete* if you are talking to more than one person)
Thank you	*Gratias ago vobis*
Yes/No	*Ita/Non*
Good/Bad	*Bonus/Malus*
I would like…	*Velim…*
How much?	*Quantus?*
How many?	*Quot?*
Where?	*Ubi?*
When?	*Quando?*
What?	*Quod?*
What is this?	*Quid hoc est?*
How much further?	*Quantus porro?*
How do I get to…?	*Qua via venio ad…?*
Is it far?	*Est ne longinquum?*
Where are the lions?	*Ubi sunt leones?*
I am hungry.	*Esurio.*
Have you got food?	*Cibum habes?*

USEFUL LATIN WORDS

FOOD AND SHOPPING

Baker	*Pistrinum*
Bread	*Panis*
Butcher	*Laniena*
Cheese	*Caseus*
Eggs	*Ova*
Fish	*Piscis*
Fruit	*Pomum*
Lettuce	*Lactuca*
Meat	*Caro*
Milk	*Lac*
Sausage	*Botulus*
Vegetables	*Holera*
Water	*Aqua*

DAYS OF THE WEEK

For most ancient Romans the day goes from midnight to midnight. However, for some people, especially visitors from Greece and Egypt, the day goes from sunrise to sunrise. If you have to be somewhere, be sure you know how to tell the time.

ROMAN DAY	MEANING	YOUR DAY
Dies Solis	Day of the Sun	Sunday
Dies Lunae	Day of the Moon	Monday
Dies Martis	Day of Mars	Tuesday
Dies Mercuris	Day of Mercury	Wednesday
Dies Iovis	Day of Jupiter	Thursday
Dies Veneris	Day of Venus	Friday
Dies Saturni	Day of Saturn	Saturday

ROMAN NUMBERS

Roman numerals (numbers) are made up from combinations of seven letters, as follows:

I = 1   V = 5   X = 10   L = 50   C = 100   D = 500   M = 1,000

It's easy enough to remember what each letter stands for, but it can get complicated when you need to write large numbers, or do addition or subtraction. When writing a number, the rules are these:

1 Numerals are written in a line.
2 Numerals start with the biggest numeral and work down to the smallest.

Here's two examples of how the numbering system works in Roman numerals:

• LXXXVIII 50 + 10 + 10 + 10 + 5 + 1 + 1 + 1 = 88
• LXXXIX   50 + 10 + 10 + 10 + (10-1) = 89

ANCIENT ROMAN NUMBERS

Number	Numeral	Latin name	Number	Numeral	Latin name
1	I	unus	20	XX	viginti
2	II	duo	30	XXX	triginta
3	III	tres	40	XL	quadraginta
4	IV	quattuor	50	L	quinquaginta
5	V	quinque	100	C	centum
6	VI	sex	200	CC	decenti
7	VII	septem	300	CCC	trecenti
8	VIII	octo	400	CD	quadringenti
9	IX	novem	500	D	quingenti
10	X	decem	1,000	M	mille

FESTIVALS AND GLADIATORS

OTHER ANCIENT ROMAN FESTIVALS

Month	Festival name	Festival description
February	*Parentalia*	In honour of family ancestors.
March	*Fordicidia*	Marks the start of the farming year.
June	*Vestalia*	In honour of Vesta, goddess of home and hearth.
August	*Portunalia*	In honour of Portunus, god of the harbour of Rome.
October	*Fontinalia*	Festival of water, in honour of Fons, god of fountains and springs.
November	*Ludi Plebeii*	Festival of games.

GLADIATORS – THE ONES TO WATCH

- **Andabata** ("blind-fighter") – wears **chain mail** and a helmet with no eye-holes. Finds his enemy by groping around.
- **Hoplomachus** ("shield-fighter") – heavily-armoured, carries a tiny round shield, and fights with a **lance** and a short sword.
- **Laquerarius** ("noose-fighter") – fights with a lasso.
- **Retiarius** ("net-fighter") – fights with a net, a three-pronged **trident**, and a long dagger.
- **Secutor** ("chaser") – carries a large rectangular shield and fights with a dagger or short sword.

ANCIENT ROME AT A GLANCE

TIMELINE

about 1000 BC	First villages on the hills of Rome.
753 BC	Legendary founding of Rome.
about 753–509 BC	Rome ruled by kings.
509 BC	Last king overthrown; Roman Republic begins.
390 BC	Rome sacked by Gauls.
264 BC	First gladiatorial contest in Rome.
264–146 BC	Wars against North Africa and Greece.
73–71 BC	Spartacus, a slave gladiator, leads a rebellion of 90,000 slaves against the Romans.
59–51 BC	Gaul is conquered.
45 BC	Caesar becomes dictator of Rome.
44 BC	Caesar assassinated for being too powerful.
27 BC	Roman Republic ends. Octavian becomes the first Roman emperor (Augustus). Roman Empire begins.
AD 43	Conquest of Britain begins.
AD 60	Queen Boudicca leads a rebellion in Britain against the Roman invaders.
AD 64	Fire destroys much of Rome; Nero begins persecution of Christians.
AD 68–69	Nero dies. Power struggles lead to civil war.
AD 79	Destruction of Roman towns by the eruption of the volcano Vesuvius.
AD 80	Colosseum opens in Rome.
about AD 120	Roman Empire at its greatest extent.
AD 120–128	Hadrian's Wall built in Britain.
AD 284	Roman Empire split into Eastern and Western parts.
AD 313	Edict of Milan: Christianity and other religions are tolerated throughout the Roman Empire.

AD 326	Constantine abolishes gladiatorial contests. (They were revived by later emperors.)
AD 330	Constantinople (Istanbul) becomes the "New Rome" in the east, capital of the Roman world.
about AD 400	Last known gladiatorial contest at the Colosseum.
AD 410	Rome sacked by Goths.
AD 476	Abdication of Romulus Augustulus, last emperor of the Western Empire.
AD 476–1453	Eastern Empire flourishes for 1,000 years, until Constantinople is conquered by the Turks.

FURTHER READING

BOOKS

Ancient Rome, Peter Connolly and Andrew Solway (Oxford University Press, 2001)

Illustrated Encyclopedia of Ancient Rome, Mike Corbishley (British Museum, 2003)

WEBSITES

- www.thebritishmuseum.ac.uk/world/rome/rome.html
  Search for items in the British Museum collection.

- www.maquettes-historiques.net/P5.html
  Superb model of the City of Rome – don't miss this one!

- www.crystalinks.com/romeclothing.html
  Clothes in ancient Rome.

GLOSSARY

altar table used for offering sacrifices and other gifts to the gods

ancestor family member who lived in the past

arcades covered passages with shops along one side

archaeologist person who studies the past by digging up the remains of ancient people and places

assassinate to kill an important person

astronomy study of the stars and planets and their movements

auction sale in which items are sold to the highest bidders

banquet great feast with many different courses of food

blacksmith person who works with iron

chain mail body armour made from small pieces of overlapping metal

chariot type of fast-moving wheeled vehicle

condemned when a person is found guilty by a court and given a punishment

dialect the different ways people pronounce words in the same language

empire group of countries all ruled by the same government

family tree all the people who are related to each other within a family, going back over many years

forum open space in a town or city, where public meetings, festivals, and processions are held

general leader in charge of the army

gladiator man trained to fight in a certain way for public entertainment

impalement being stuck on a sharp object

jury group of people at a trial who decide whether a person is guilty or not guilty of a crime

lame unable to walk normally because of an injured foot or leg

lance long pole with a pointed end used as a weapon

litter type of seat for a single person carried by a group of bearers on their shoulders

lucky charm small object carried or worn by a person and which they believe will bring them good luck

magistrate official who listens to a court case and decides what should happen to a person charged with a crime

mosaic picture on the floor or wall made from small pieces of coloured stone, glass, or clay

multicultural society in which people of all races and religions live together

niche (in a building) slot for a statue to stand inside

pagan person who does not believe in the main religion of the country in which they live

persecute to be cruel to people, especially because of their beliefs

prophecy telling the future

proverb well-known saying that states the truth or gives advice

republic government in which ordinary people choose their leaders

resin sticky sap from trees

sacred place or object that is considered to be holy

sacrifice offerings made to a god, such as food, and particularly an animal killed for the purpose

senator member of the Senate, which was the governing body of Rome

sulphur pale yellow substance that burns with a blue flame and makes a strong smell

temple building used for religious ceremonies

toga standard item of clothing for men for much of Roman history

trident three-pronged fork used to spear fish, and as a weapon by some gladiators

INDEX

Titles in the *Time Travel Guides* series include:

ANCIENT
CHINA

Hardback 978-1-406-20601-2

ANCIENT
ROME

Hardback 978-1-406-20599-2

ANCIENT
EGYPT

Hardback 978-1-406-20600-5

THE
AZTEC
EMPIRE

Hardback 978-1-406-20602-9

ANCIENT
GREECE

Hardback 978-1-406-20598-5

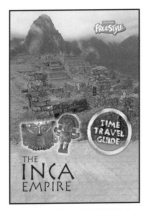

THE
INCA
EMPIRE

Hardback 978-1-406-20603-6

Find out about the other titles in this series on our website www.raintreepublishers.co.uk